Happy
Travels .

Cheers
Tracy

DIMITRI DISCOVERS™

ENGLAND

By
Tracy Langley
DLB Publishing

DLB Publishing
San Jose, California 95117
Copyright 2006 ©
All rights reserved.

Distributed in Europe by C. Grange
Hemel Hempstead, Hertfordshire, England HP24NY

Distributed in Asia by S. Hicks
Shuguang Xili Chaoyang District 100028 Beijing China

Distributed in North America by M. Lanz
Kingston Road, Toronto, ON, M1N 4E2, Canada

Distributed in Australia by M. Saunders
Cromer Heights, NSW 2099, Sydney, Australia.

Distributed in South America by D. Armas
Campo Alegre, Quito, Ecuador, South America

British Library Cataloguing in Publication Data.
Langley, Tracy—Dimitri Discovers England: a book of adventure and learning.
1. England—Description and Travel—Juvenile Literature I. Title 914.2'0486—B5N79

Library of Congress Control Number 2007904583
Dimitri Discovers England/by Tracy Langley
Summary: Dimitri discovers points of interest, differences and a bit of fun in England.
{1. Children's Stories 2. Travel 3. Photography 4. History}

ISBN 978-0-9793150-0-8
First Published in 2008
Composed in California, USA
Regal Printing Limited China

'This charming book had me smiling at the first page. Fun to look at and engaging to read, it will delight both children and adults."
— Kathleen Ann Gonzalez, author of Free Gondola Ride
www.freegondolaride.com

'Descubrir lugares nuevos, conocer gente nueva y comprender diferencias es fundamental para el desarrollo de los niños. Dimitri Descubre es una aventura basada en una historia de la vida real que incluye hechos divertidos."
—Susanna Dorn, directora y fundadora de "Juguemos en Espanol"
www.juguemosenespanol.com

'Discovering new places, meeting new people and understanding differences is important to all children's development! Dimitri Discovers is a real life adventure story with fun facts included."
— Susanna Dorn, Director and Founder "Let's Play In Spanish"
www.letsplayinspanish.com

Foreword

Dimitri Discovers England

Here's a book about Dimitri's expedition across the Atlantic Ocean. When you have read it, I hope you and your family will also want to come and visit us and explore England yourself.

Travel is great. You discover exciting new places and people. You learn about the ways people live in different parts of our wide world. You can make new friends and sometimes maybe find out that some things aren't too different from the way they are at home.

On his trip Dimitri found out about England's history, our culture, how we spend our leisure time, and about famous places to visit. I'm glad his trip took him to the Palace of Westminster in London where our Parliament is located – and where I work.

Dimitri, his mum Tracy Langley, and I are cousins. Over the years, like Tracy, many of our family members have left England to settle in other parts of the world, some of them nearly 100 years ago when traveling wasn't as easy as it usually is now. South Africa, Australia, and Canada as well as the US are just some of the countries where we have other cousins.

Maybe one day we'll have the chance to meet them all. In the meantime, enjoy the book and happy traveling!

David Lepper

David Lepper MP
United Kingdom Parliament
www.parliament.uk

DEDICATED TO MY MUM WHO BROUGHT A LITTLE PIECE OF ENGLAND TO ME EVERY DAY...

BERYL LANGLEY
OCTOBER 30, 1937 – JANUARY 26, 2005

Come discover England with me.
It's as easy as one, two, three!

London Taxi

Double-Decker Bus

Sightseeing Cruise

The "Tube"

DID YOU KNOW?

YOU CAN WALK, TAKE THE UNDERGROUND TRAIN, A TAXI, A DOUBLE-DECKER BUS, OR A CRUISE BOAT TO SEE LONDON. THE LONDON UNDERGROUND HAS MORE THAN 250 MILES OF TRACK, AND MORE THAN HALF OF THE ENTIRE SYSTEM IS ABOVE GROUND. THE NICKNAME "TUBE" COMES FROM THE ALMOST CIRCULAR, TUBE-LIKE TUNNELS THROUGH WHICH THE SMALL TRAINS TRAVEL.

With so much to see,
There is no time for a nap.
Take the tube to Tower Bridge,
And, oh yes, 'Mind the gap!'

Tower Bridge on the River Thames

Follow Signs to the Tube

London Bridge now in Havasu City, Arizona USA

Tower Bridge with Bascules Open

DID YOU KNOW?

YOU CAN TAKE THE TUBE FROM PADDINGTON STATION VIA MOORGATE TO LONDON BRIDGE STATION TO GET TO TOWER BRIDGE. IN 1968, ROBERT P. MCCULLOUGH BOUGHT THE LONDON BRIDGE FOR $2,500,000 AND MOVED IT TO LAKE HAVASU, ARIZONA.

We visit the Tower of London
To view the Crown Jewels.
They are only worn by the Queen,
If anyone asks you...she rules!

Yeoman Warder or Beefeaters

British Crown

Tower of London

Jewel Tower

DID YOU KNOW?

THE CROWN JEWELS INCLUDE THE QUEEN'S CROWN, SCEPTERS, SWORDS, AND RINGS. YEARS AGO, THE CROWN JEWELS WERE KEPT AT WESTMINSTER ABBEY, BUT SOMEONE STOLE THEM! THEY ARE NOW UNDER GUARD IN THE TOWER OF LONDON. BEEFEATERS ARE CEREMONIAL GUARDIANS OF THE TOWER OF LONDON AND IN SEPTEMBER 2007, THE FIRST WOMAN BEEFEATER WAS ON GUARD.

Off to the Bank of England
To pick up some money.
The British call their money 'pounds'.
I think that is funny!

Bank of England

My Money Bank

English £10 Pound Note

EURO Currency

Threadneedle Street

DID YOU KNOW?

AT SOME DATE IN THE FUTURE, ENGLAND MAY SWITCH ITS CURRENCY FROM THE BRITISH POUND TO THE EURO. THE EURO IS WHAT ALL EUROPEAN UNION COUNTRIES USE AS A COMMON CURRENCY.

Let's feed all the birds
At St. Paul's Cathedral.
It is just a short walk
Down the road from Threadneedle.

St. Paul's Cathedral

St. Paul's Cathedral

St. Paul's Clock
Tower

St. Paul's Cathedral

DID YOU KNOW?

ST. PAUL'S CATHEDRAL HAS BEEN FEATURED IN MANY FAMOUS MOVIES INCLUDING MARY POPPINS, PETER PAN, AND 101 DALMATIANS. A SHORT CLIMB OF 530 STEPS WILL BRING YOU TO THE TOP TO SEE ALL OF LONDON AND THE THAMES. BE SURE TO SIT AND WHISPER IN THE WHISPERING GALLERY. YOU WILL NOT REGRET IT.

Juggler

Part of the Balloon Show

There is always something cool
Going on at Covent Garden.
To get through the crowds
Say 'excuse me' and 'pardon'.

Punch and Judy

Live Statue

DID YOU KNOW?

AT COVENT GARDEN THERE ARE STREET PER-
FORMERS PRACTICING MAGIC, JUGGLING,
AND PUTTING ON PUPPET SHOWS. ONE OF
THE FIRST SHOWS IN COVENT GARDEN WAS
THE "PUNCH AND JUDY" PUPPET SHOW IN
1662.

Mr. William Shakespeare
Was a great English writer.
But at my age
I like my stories a bit lighter.

Globe Theater Stage

Globe Theater Balcony

Mr. Shakespeare

DID YOU KNOW?

WILLIAM SHAKESPEARE WAS AN ENGLISH POET AND PLAYWRIGHT WIDELY REGARDED AS THE GREATEST WRITER OF THE ENGLISH LANGUAGE. HIS WORK INCLUDES 37 PLAYS INCLUDING ROMEO AND JULIET, MACBETH, HAMLET, AND A MIDSUMMER NIGHT'S DREAM. HE ALSO WROTE 154 SONNETS, WHICH ARE POEMS CONTAINING EXACTLY 14 LINES EACH.

Globe Theater Open-Air Ceiling

Trafalgar Fountain

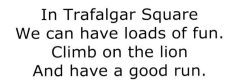

In Trafalgar Square
We can have loads of fun.
Climb on the lion
And have a good run.

Climb on the Lion!

Nelson's Column

DID YOU KNOW?
IN 2003, A LAW WAS PASSED
MAKING IT ILLEGAL TO FEED THE
PIGEONS IN TRAFALGAR SQUARE.

Trafalgar Square

Seven floors of great toys
Await at Hamley's toy store.
We will shop on all seven
And still want to play more!

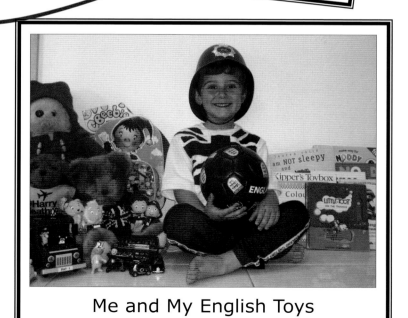

Hamley's Toy Store

Regent Street

DID YOU KNOW?

YOU CAN CATCH A DOUBLE-DECKER BUS TO HAMLEY'S TOY STORE ON REGENT STREET AND SHOP FOR YOUR FAVORITE ENGLISH TOYS. HAMLEY'S TOY STORE USED TO BE CALLED "NOAH'S ARK" IN 1760, AND NOW IT HAS ABOUT FIVE MILLION VISITORS A YEAR.

Me and My English Toys

Buckingham Palace

Sitting still at Buckingham Palace
Can be very hard,
But it is all worth it to see
The changing of the guard.

Changing of the Guard

The Queen Returning Home

DID YOU KNOW?
YOU WALK THROUGH GREEN PARK TO BUCKINGHAM PALACE. BUCKINGHAM PALACE IS THE OFFICIAL HOME TO THE QUEEN. THERE ARE MORE THAN 500 ROOMS AND 78 BATHROOMS IN THE PALACE.

Me at the Palace Gate

To get to Kensington Palace,
We stroll through Hyde Park.
It has been a long day already,
And it is getting a bit dark.

Kensington Palace

Marble Arch

DID YOU KNOW?

TAKE THE TUBE TO MARBLE ARCH STATION, THEN WALK THROUGH HYDE PARK TO GET TO KENSINGTON PALACE. THE GARDENS AND PALACE ARE A GREAT PLACE TO RUN AND PLAY, AND YOU WILL SEE A STATUE OF PETER PAN AND THE ALBERT MEMORIAL. DIANA, PRINCESS OF WALES, OCCUPIED APARTMENTS AT KENSINGTON PALACE FROM 1981 TO 1997.

Albert Memorial

Peter Pan Statue

Westminster Abbey
North Entrance

Mom snaps a picture of me
Posing under the archway.
Instead of taking pictures,
Let's run, jump, and play!

Statues above the Great West Door

Westminster Abbey

DID YOU KNOW?
TEN 20TH-CENTURY CHRISTIAN
MARTYRS, INCLUDING DR. MARTIN
LUTHER KING, JR., ARE DEPICTED
IN STATUES ABOVE THE GREAT
WEST DOOR OF WESTMINSTER
ABBEY.

Me at Westminster Abbey

Around and around
Big Ben we played,
Then over to the House of Parliament
Where the English laws are made.

Westminster Palace

Big Ben

Face of Big Ben

Victoria Tower

DID YOU KNOW?

YOU WALK OVER THE ROAD TO WESTMINSTER PALACE, THE HOUSE OF PARLIAMENT, VICTORIA TOWER, THE CLOCK NAMED "BIG BEN". BIG BEN IS A 316-FOOT-HIGH CLOCK TOWER AND IS THE WORLD'S LARGEST FOUR-FACED CHIMING CLOCK. THE HOUR HAND ON THE CLOCK IS NINE FEET LONG, AND THE MINUTE HAND IS 14 FEET LONG.

London Eye Observation "Pod"

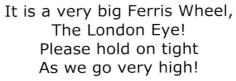

It is a very big Ferris Wheel,
The London Eye!
Please hold on tight
As we go very high!

London Eye Over London

The View from the Top

London Eye

DID YOU KNOW?

THE LONDON EYE, ALSO KNOWN AS THE MILLENIUM WHEEL, OPENED IN 1999 AND IS THE LARGEST OBSERVATION WHEEL IN THE WORLD. MORE PEOPLE RIDE THE LONDON EYE EVERY YEAR THAN VISIT THE STATUE OF LIBERTY, LEANING TOWER OF PISA, AND THE EIFFEL TOWER ... OVER 3.5 MILLION VISITORS A YEAR.

Back to Tower Bridge
On our River Thames cruise.
The captain says hurry!
The bridge may 'close' soon!

Under the Tower Bridge

Tower Bridge Closed

Tower Bridge Open

DID YOU KNOW?

THE TOWER BRIDGE BEGAN OPERATION IN 1894 AND TOOK OVER EIGHT YEARS TO BUILD. THE BASCULES ARE RAISED AND LOWERED OVER 900 TIMES A YEAR; THAT'S ABOUT THREE TIMES A DAY.

Me and My Paddington

At the Paddington Station
We end our day.
I ring my dad back home.
He is in! Hurray!!!

Red Phone Box

Calling Home
From a Black
Phone Box

Paddington Bear at the Station

DID YOU KNOW?

HISTORIC PADDINGTON STATION WAS PART OF THE WORLD'S FIRST UNDERGROUND RAILWAY BACK IN 1838. PADDINGTON BEAR IS SAID TO BE FROM DEEPEST, DARKEST PERU. THE RED TELEPHONE BOX CAN BE SEEN THROUGHOUT THE UNITED KINGDOM AND MALTA.

Touring Windsor Castle,
The guard stands like a tree.
We took loads of photos.
Can you find one of me?

The Round Tower

Inside Windsor Castle

Windsor Castle Changing of the Guard

Me and the Guard

DID YOU KNOW?
WINDSOR CASTLE IS WHERE THE QUEEN LIVES ON THE WEEKEND. WINDSOR CASTLE IS THE LARGEST INHABITED CASTLE IN THE WORLD, AND IT IS THE OLDEST IN CONTINUOUS OCCUPATION. THE GUARDS ARE NOT ALLOWED TO MOVE OR TALK TO YOU WHEN THEY ARE ON DUTY!

A View from Guy's Tower

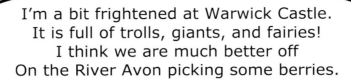
I'm a bit frightened at Warwick Castle.
It is full of trolls, giants, and fairies!
I think we are much better off
On the River Avon picking some berries.

A Troll!!

Guy's Tower and Courtyard

Me at Warwick Castle

DID YOU KNOW?

AT WARWICK CASTLE YOU CAN DISCOVER THE DUNGEONS AND TOWERS. WARWICK CASTLE WAS ORIGINALLY BUILT IN 914 BY ETHELFLEDA, THE DAUGHTER OF KING ALFRED THE GREAT. SCALE THE TOWERS AND EXPLORE THE 60 ACRES OF FUN. SEE A JOUSTING TOURNAMENT, BIRDS OF PREY, AND KNIGHTS IN ACTION.

Mom says St. Albans
Is quite important in history.
To me, it is just good fun;
All the rest is just a mystery.

Inside St. Albans Abbey

View of St. Albans

DID YOU KNOW?

ONE OF THE FIRST DRAFTS OF THE MAGNA CARTA, CONSIDERED ONE OF THE MOST IMPORTANT LEGAL DOCUMENTS IN THE HISTORY OF DEMOCRACY, WAS DRAFTED AT ST. ALBANS ABBEY.
DECEMBER 10, 2007, A COPY OF THE MAGNA CARTA WAS UP FOR AUCTION AT SOTHEBY'S AND IT WAS SOLD FOR $20+ MILLION.

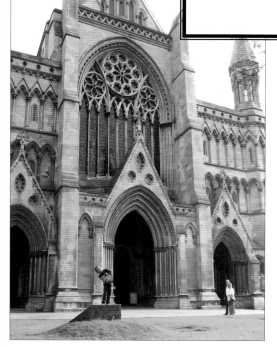

Front of the Abbey

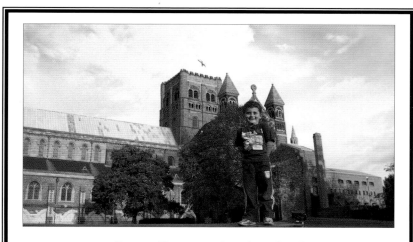

St. Albans Cathedral

Stonehenge

Stonehenge is an ancient monument
Made of very old stones from Wales.
Why is it there, and what does it mean?
I have heard loads of tales.

Stonehenge

Stonehenge

DID YOU KNOW?

STONEHENGE IS A COLLECTION OF VERY OLD AND BIG STANDING STONES STICKING OUT OF THE GROUND IN WILTSHIRE, ENGLAND. ARCHAEOLOGISTS BELIEVE THAT THE STANDING STONES AT STONEHENGE WERE ERECTED BETWEEN 2500 AND 2000 B.C., WHICH WOULD MAKE THEM MORE THAN 4,000 YEARS OLD.

In England there are many things
To see and play and do.
And I did most of them
Before the ripe old age of two!

Cricket Match

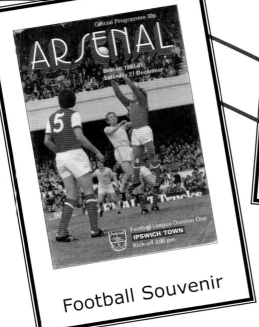

Football Souvenir

Horse Racing

Football (Soccer) Match

Rugby

DID YOU KNOW?

HERE ARE SOME OF THE SPORTS WE DISCOVERED IN ENGLAND. A CRICKET MATCH CAN LAST FOR SIX OR MORE HOURS A DAY FOR UP TO FIVE DAYS! DURING THE MATCH, THE PLAYERS TAKE BREAKS FOR TEA AND LUNCH.

The kids call their mommy "mum,"
Some roofs are made of straw,
Cars drive on the left-
Those are just some differences I saw!

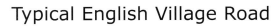

Typical English Village Road

Me and My Mates

Fish and Chips

Anne Hathaway's Cottage
Stratford-upon-Avon

DID YOU KNOW?

ICONS OF ENGLAND INCLUDE JAMES BOND, ALICE IN WONDERLAND, THE MINISKIRT, SIR ISSAC NEWTON, THE BEATLES, CAMBRIDGE, ETON AND OXFORD UNIVERSITIES, SHERLOCK HOLMES, MONTY PYTHON, ROBIN HOOD, FISH AND CHIPS, CHARLES DARWIN, THE OXFORD ENGLISH DICTIONARY, THE MINI, ROLLS-ROYCE, WIMBLEDON, WINNIE THE POOH, NODDY, BOB THE BUILDER, THOMAS THE TANK ENGINE, BEATRIX POTTER, SIR RICHARD BRANSON, HARRY POTTER, GUY RITCHIE, DAVID AND VICTORIA BECKHAM, AND MANY MORE!

Seeing new signs and learning new words
While you are walking about.
But what do these signs really mean
And can YOU figure them out?

Tube Station Sign

Low Ceiling

Watch Your Step

Form a Line

Exit

Street Sign

Catch a Taxi

DID YOU KNOW?

SOME STATION PLATFORMS ON THE LONDON UNDER-GROUND ARE CURVED. SINCE THE CARS ARE STRAIGHT, THE DISTANCE FROM THE PLATFORM TO THE CAR AT CERTAIN POINTS IS GREATER THAN NORMAL. SO THE PHRASE 'MIND THE GAP' IS PAINTED ON THE EDGE OF THE PLATFORM.

Meet the Constables

In England, there is so much to learn
And so much to do.
But I have run out of room in this book
To show them all to you.

See the Mary Poppins Play

Swordfight

Climb the Stairs at the Castle

Feed the Ducks

DID YOU KNOW?

ENGLAND HAS MANY DIFFERENT VENUES FOR TOURISM. YOU CAN WRITE, EMAIL, CALL, OR STOP AT ANY LOCAL OFFICE TO LEARN WHAT IS HAPPENING IN THE AREA. YOU CAN ICESKATE AT WINDSOR, HYDE PARK, OR THE TOWER OF LONDON DURING THE WINTER. YOU CAN VISIT NATIONAL PARKS OR WORLD HERITAGE SITES AND TAKE COUNTRYSIDE WALKS.

Post a Letter

I take a map on every adventure;
It is a great learning tool.
With my map in my hand,
Discovering new places is so cool!

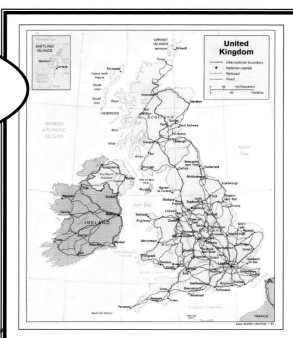

The United Kingdom

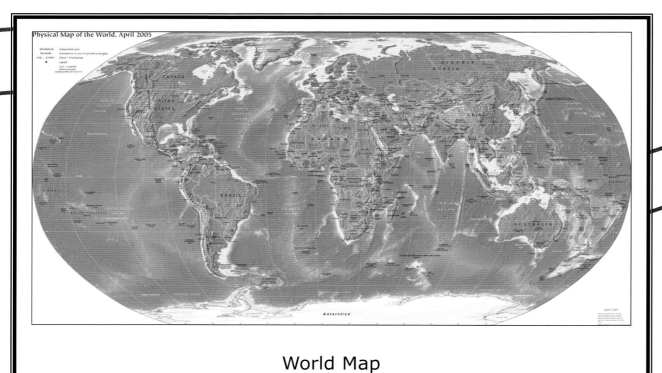

World Map

Europe

DID YOU KNOW?

THERE ARE MORE THAN SEVEN BILLION PEOPLE IN THE WORLD; MORE THAN 700 MILLION PEOPLE LIVE IN EUROPE, AND 61 MILLION PEOPLE LIVE IN THE UNITED KINGDOM. ENGLAND IS AN ISLAND AND IS PART OF THE UNITED KINGDOM.

The United Kingdom flag
Is known as the "Union Jack."
It is printed on everything,
So Mommy sewed one on my backpack!

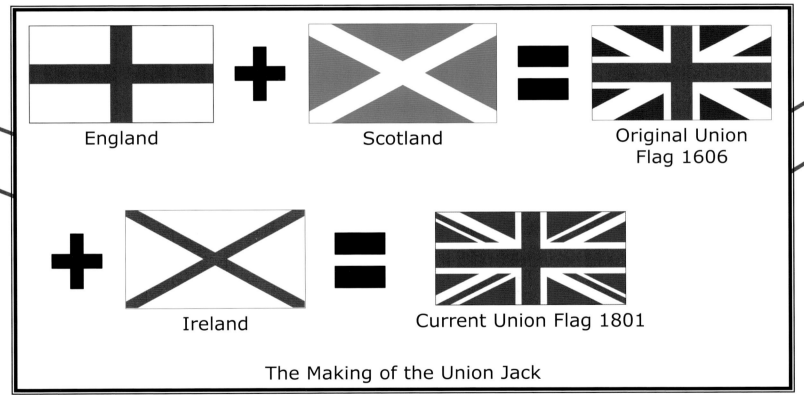

England + Scotland = Original Union Flag 1606

+ Ireland = Current Union Flag 1801

The Making of the Union Jack

DID YOU KNOW?

THE UNITED KINGDOM IS MADE UP OF ENGLAND, SCOTLAND, NORTHERN IRELAND AND WALES. THE FLAG OF THE UNITED KINGDOM IS A COMBINATION OF THE NATIONAL FLAGS OF ENGLAND, SCOTLAND, AND IRELAND.

As our adventure of England
Comes to an end,
I wish "Happy Travels"
To YOU, your family, and friends.

Thank you for discovering
England with me.
Our great big world awaits
We have many more places to see!